Honey L
Scars

Callie McDonald

Honey Laced Scars 2024

Dedicated to whoever's soft flowered palms touch the pages of this book

Starry eyed

Starry eyed, after midnight you lied

Next to me, your chestnut hair, and your laced white underwear

Green eyes, touch me with sugar-coated candy dripped lies

Cigarette, pressed against her smoke infiltrated lips

Melted honey, between her legs drips

Stardust bliss, starry eyed and chocolate kissed

She tastes like strawberries and mist

My love is buried In Vancouver

I wish to be strangled with gentle hands

So, when daylight touches my ivory skin, same story, different man

The crucified corpse, buried with obliterated remorse

Detoxing off of love, beloved fake God above

With blisters on his thumbs, Oh how we are dumb

Now he is buried in Vancouver

His corpse rotting in a love potion mixture, and his limbs in the trunk of an Uber

Biopsy

I danced with wildflowers over a dazzling scarlet haze

Biopsy, razor blades, and beautiful things glaze

They pried me open with a disease

Biopsy, wildflower breeze

They dissected my limbs and covered them with a paper cast

Biopsy was signed with a sharpie and flowers sewed into the wound that would last

Lilith

Reduced to skin and bone
Pink silky dresses flown
Floral patterns laced white
Ribbons tied around her hair in twilight
The ocean sea waves crashing in
Ruffles trace her skin
My strawberries and wine
Beautiful grapes upon her vine
Step forward and let the rain wash down
Wear your hand-me-down gown
Lilith, please stay around

Paper replicas

I wanna rip my organs out and replace them with paper replicas

Because when they speak it's like their poking my pores

The ability to feel clean

The ability to make things dirty

The ability to feel like I'm more

The urge I have to become a mother, to love everything that doesn't seem loved

To comfort and to care when no one else does

I need love because I am full of it, does one deserve reconsideration?

For I love a simple creature not worthy of anything but abuse

I will comfort and care for it like it needs, but not deserves

I will speak true words

But words I speak because I need to, because I love this grisly leach

It is mine, no one else, for it is me

Twilight

Do you hear the crawling of broken limbs cracking in the twilight sky?

Where angels leap and rip themselves apart limb from limb, beauty in their Bambi eyes

Watery tears forming at the seeping whole of gore, as beautiful as flesh, all was before

The carnage of what's left of the corpse, I choose to ignore

And flowers spurt from the raw scalping of a beautiful whore

The frigid twilight haze and a cashmere sweater she wore, tore

Garden of Eden

Baby, sweet like hard candy
My silky sheets left sandy
My lover, walk with me in gardens of Eden
Let me flourish let me sweeten
Periwinkles and passion flowers
I stare at my marble ceiling for hours
I lay in a bed of daisies and tulips
Weeds and seeds that I already threw up
And now I have sinned, my love isn't something all within
But only undercovers, in the sheets forever

Rosemary fields

Lay with skin bare eating flowers

Thinking upon hours of hours until I feel sour

Praying to my porcelain goddess, contemplating if this is who I am, a man and your dog that I am

Infected I do and through I spew the words into sending a love above

My porcelain goddess hovers and gutters at the mothers of lovers beneath her

She cries and lies, knowing she will never be and see what a man is to be

Rosemary and thyme, the church bell chimes, I never got to say goodbye

As I lay in a field chewing on roses and hair, unaware

Sick animal

Like a sick animal, I love you

With a disease, foaming at my mouth, rabid and unafraid

Tasting your flesh, with my pale pink lips

I bite your bruised knees and hips

And now what was pretty, is pulverized

You'll have to sew yourself back together with broken blades

As I cling onto all your remains

Is it because she's like me?

He sees me because he has eyes, not because he
wants to love someone new

And my mother doesn't need me, so now the only color
in my life is the stained sheets on my bed

The petals in the garden are painted red by gunshot
wounds to the head

Why do you love her now?

Is it because she's like me?

Dog bait

Empty, I am Empty

I am an animal, a sickness and I am rage

A drug capsule, a rubber band

Your hand you use me, and expect me to stay?

I love everyone I date, I am dog bait

I bite that hand, the one that feeds

Tainted meat, I bite myself till I bleed

My collar of sin, waiting till I feed

Hungry, I am born hungry, longing for something,
anything, I'm hungry

Love

Peering over the balcony

Feet dangling over the edge

Pretty images and scrimmages of delusions within my head

Spilling my guts is the only love I've known at night, when I lay down on the bed

An idea, a feeling, a thought, and a dread

A talentless name that I feel to me is dead

A lonely meaningless beg for you, even though we are through, its name is love

It's all I can think of

Cherry lip gloss

Dark circles under my eyes and cherry lip gloss
White dresses, pink laces, and candy floss
Sandy seashores, and dazzling hues
Radiant things, summer blues
And now my heart strings are being pulled apart
Veins and all, like an art
Vandalize my mind and soul
I know it is your beautiful goal
So, I kiss your face with my cherry-stained lips
As tears run down like waves crashing into ships

Chocolate kiss

Chocolate kiss, forever bliss
I love the one, I won't get to miss
I'm boring and tired
My heart is ripped and wired
I love you but I’m not your desire
Chocolate kiss, forever bliss
I hate the one that I might miss.
My heart is sewn and threaded
Feelings and thoughts, I have dreaded
A beautiful art, silhouetted
Chocolate kiss

Fluent

I am only fluent in apologizing
The words that linger in my mouth stay stapled
I want to peel my nerves back from their flesh
Refill myself with filth and things that I am capable
To be loved it's like being faulted
It's like being violent, isn't it?
Like a disease, it spreads through nerves
I know what to say but, I don't have the words

You don't understand me

Silhouettes of the seashore glisten

Pretty pillows, lay on them you never seem to listen

I love you, but you don't understand me

I can't keep calm I can't keep quiet; I was born to be free

And now bittersweet bubblegum has a tangy taste on my teeth

Melancholic things that lay beneath, pressure and persuade their way, into a woman's heart who wonders and wishes she was art

And the beach moves hauntingly, daunting me with it's beautiful parts

I love you, but you don't understand me

I love you, but you don't understand

me

Cinnamon

Spill a drink from the coffee table,

cinnamon, and tea

Beautiful view, ocean lidocaine sea

Sunday's sun rays shine down, I still miss you even when you're around.

Now the white carpets stained

Alluring feelings I haven't gained

Sometimes I wonder if it's better when your gone

Innocent like a blood-stained fawn, I believe your lies

Through beautiful azure, blue, blue eyes

Cinnamon taste on my lips, tea drips from my narrow hips

Let death be kinder than I am

Let death be kinder than I am

For I cannot bear that I am becoming less interesting

Will you still want to be in my presence even when I'm nothing new?

Let death be kinder than I am

44, Beautiful from afar

I thought you would fill the whole of me

But your just like every person I've loved

You only want me when there's nothing to give

I'll eat my own spit and puke up my own acids

Empty myself of my mistake

But I can't say much

Because I love someone new every day

I can't control myself of my irregularities

I can't manage to love myself

For what is there to love if you don't regard for my flaws

So, I'm gagging on my own laced stitches and my stomach wounds are pried open

And I've taken about 44 melatonin to help me sleep it off

The world is beautiful from afar

44 pills and it's still beautiful from my view

Papercuts

Quiet blue water, I’m chasing paper airplanes

Paper heart and paper brain, rip me apart with teeth and taste my veins

I am human, flesh and skin, bones, and all

Love me till I sin, love me till I fall

And if I fall would you catch me?

And if you wouldn't I'd finally be free

And now I have paper cuts on my hands and knees

As I lay naked in the cold breeze

Blooming bouquets

Blooming bouquets of blossoming bluebells blow in their
ballad of Melancholia

Pretty purple petunias shine in shimmering sunlight like
a melodrama

Perfect petals of painted pink daisies dance like two
lovers

Orchids ostracize their leaves in changing colors

Numbers and letters, colors, and seasons, all remind me
of recurring remembrances

I still remember the flowers you gave me like an
inconvenience

Blackbirds

Perfect petals punctuate the floorboards

Strumming strings, bruised fingers bleeding from chords

And now what was pretty is bent backwards

The watercolor sky fades with flying shot down blackbirds

Their wings plucked from their roots and their flesh all over the room

Death is beautiful all in bloom

I couldn't say no

Why do I have to be the example settler?

Can't I be the weak one for once?

I love like a dog, I won't make a fuss

I want you to feel my rage, get me out of this cage

Feel my hate and sorrow throw me out till tomorrow

There's a chain around my neck getting tighter and tighter

my love isn't something you can just borrow

I asked you if it was my fault and you said, "I don't know," even though he played with my skin like playdough

I should say no

I should've said no, I could've said no

I can't say no

I couldn't say no

Was I frozen? My body attracted your eyes

Look Down my legs and thighs

I should say no

I should've said no

I could've said no

I can't say no

I couldn't say no

I was frozen

Suffering is love

Snap my neck and call it an act of love
And let me still love you even if it hurts
Suffering is love
And I let all the love rot inside me

Orgasmic bluebells

I want your hands down my pants till I'm cumming flowers

Tangy taste on my lips sticky and wet, devoured

Your hands show how much you love

Each curve your fingers trace, my silky lace flowing above

Flowers like prostitutes, shining in glimmering moonlight

Orgasmic bluebells, in radiant twilight

Cherry flavored antidote

Gentle morning rot, blossom brings harmony

Cherry flavored antidote, blood like liquid bleeding from arteries

I am plagued by nothing at all, but crimson dreams and re-opening wounds

Swimming in cherry dark bloodstream lagoons

Violence

It's like the first taste of dried blood from picking your lips
raw, fresh, and heavy

Coming in like a summers warm kiss, scorching your
skin

Making you peel it back from flesh and root,

till it drips bliss

You'll never forget how he touched you, plucked the
roses from your body, how he wanted to touch your
flower and plant his roots in the embodiment of you

And once I rid myself of the mess, I went back to the
only thing I knew, the only way I knew how to love,
violence

Skinny

I am always hungry, filling my stomach with waters and acids to relieve the feeling

Cigarettes and glass to stop the craving

Delicate diet, I'm feeding myself cherry coke and lesser things

Two fingers down my throat, gagging on my own disease

Thinner, skinned down to my stem, skinny is my plead

And I dream, dream of a weight scale breaking, the glass shards engraving themselves in me

If I got skinner, maybe my mother wouldn't want to pick out my guts with a scalpel to reshape me, skinny

Femme fatale

Femme fatale in cigarette veil

Glittered bows, of feminine woes

A Cinnamon kiss laced clothes

Bitter bliss, in cherry mist

I sleep with my hands in fists

Cherry dreams, and cigarette schemes

Coca-Cola, vaccines

Femme cattlemen, cigarette veil

My bones are bitter and frail

Cocktails and magazines, the prettiest girl you've ever seen

Wearing silk fur, torn jeans

Touched by one, means touched by many

Scrubbing off inflicted wounds till she's twenty

Femme fatale.

The heart beats the loudest

Oh, how my limbs twist in glory of a love, folded up and
put in a box filled with eyes and organs by a man
wearing satin gloves

The heart beats the loudest, thumping against the
cardboard carrier, its blood vessels begging to be put
back in

He scrapes out my guts, stitching me together to be thin

To be delicate and fragile, a product of a human man's
sins

The garbage man watches, waiting for the bag filled with
brains and shackles

My violet vessel, in a fire pit burning, crackles

The heart beats the loudest, thumping in pits of fire

The man that dissected me once loved me, but was a
liar

He tore out every bit of me he said he loved, to rebuild
me to "beauty" murmuring to me last words, "you are
now from me, beloved"

Forest fire

Bathing in baskets of roses, I sat dazzled and felt the
lather of a thousand fires touching skin

I had never felt such a hate, such a love and such a
passion before, almost like honey drenched sin

Tasting the words off your tongue and intertwining
hatred and burning desire, I felt the color red eating off
my scabs and replacing them with blood clotted wires

I'll let the blood sink into the floorboards like red wine,
while I breathe glass shards as they poke and punctuate
my neck like the grasp of your hands twisting my spine

Burning my flesh I am rottenly sun kissed, radiating an
unrequited love like getting limbs pulled apart and
bleeding while they twist.

Hate

I hate myself; I hate the way I act and how I throw up
every time a thick handful of hate gets thrown down my
throat

To joy I tether, and my ankles collapse unto pavement
scraping my knees, I’m cold I'd like to sleep in a warm
bed tonight

All my dead body flowers shall grow a big warmth of
hate

Something I'm full of something that burns and rots
away, all that Is full of love is hate

Hate, I am infiltrated with a man

I hate everything I am, so I replace it with the moving
hook of bloodstream back stabbed wounds, blood that
gushes black. A thick pool of hate, I hate my weight.
Hate.

Tired

I feel a warm disgust and hate, if I am full of love why do
I feel such hate?

I give my whole existence and in return I get a handful of
spark plugs

The electric pulse, stings and rains acids pouring down
my throat and tasting clotted truths

I am so tired, sick, and empty

The same hate over and over again and I return it with
an equal amount and become hate

I am tired

Ripped apart to the pit of my cherry

Ripped apart to the pit of my cherry

My ankles are fragile, and so are the bones in my back
from the heaviness of it all, pomegranate berries

I'm getting in my head and I'm missing you again, all
because our eyes met once, or maybe twice, stab
wounds by a pen

Felt like a chest pain, but it was just the ink spreading
You ripped me in half, glands floating like pheromones
glistening

My seed stripped from the root of me now, cherry
dripped down on the white gown

Perfectly warn down and decapitated with a paper clip

My stomach twisted in knots, insides cherry colored and
I felt the cherry pit

Stripped from the pit of me and replaced by black ink
More than friends, less than lovers, now that I think.

Twist

I twist together what doesn't mend, and it breaks, moves forward and bends

I can deplete decapitated does, roses in fields, blood stained in rows

Cut down the trees that gave you air, then you can choke on your own bruising

Then we can have the same wounds shared

I empty-handed the only love that I know, going back to the only thing that could show

My blood-stained hands grabbed the body with delicate whispers, they murmured "It's time to go home" as he strips her

Take her down to the field, let her drip all over it as she is honey suckle laced and cocaine traced

Peeling back with fingers, her face

Twisting the limb and honey drips low, lovely price but a heavy tow.

Mother

Mother Kissing you till your lips fall off, like you're the only thing I've ever tasted

I smoke away my feelings, doesn't it remind you of someone father, turning into my mother what a life she wasted

"I'm not like her"

I repeat to all my blood spilling

But when I look through the reflection in the mirror I see my mother, I must need a new pill bottle refilling

I know he sees her in me too, my lover when I taste him

I feel the starvation take my breath and I let the sound fill my ears with honey

Mother, take my hand again and love me more than your pill capsules, I'll pay you good money

To be held in your arms once more and be moon kissed and forever hollow, to hear "I'll love always, forever and again till tomorrow"

"Mother, your love can I borrow?"

The Steakhouse

Daisys plucked bleeding down now frowning faces
around breathing in her

Feeding off the dogs canines, chewing down on bitter
veins and torn fur

Cannibalism, like candy and bleeding birds

Stapled mouth,11 words

Sugarcane and tasty steakhouse worms

I like you better when we're on bad terms

Steakhouse frying the burnt appendix of death and
rotting lilac, I feel the pretty pink veins crack

Now all is in nothing looking back, tasting your lavender
plague me in a bloomed trap

Angels porn

Dull white and glitter body cream, rubbing it deeper into
the cut that was split open with scissors so then I could
feel clean

I then ripped apart all that was left so it would consume
itself to nothing

Burning like raw milk and angels porn, acid loving

Brittle white bones chewed through her pale skin and
blue ribboned dress

Biting down on weed laced cookies, teacups and
needles that needed to be digest

I decorated with pretty pink balloons and white roses,
perfect pill bottle doses

Cigarette smoked with my skin as the paper, I wonder if
you feel bad for raping her

I suppose heaven likes it as it is angels porn, a child
stripped down and decapitated with men watching
around her like never before

Bleeding doe bloody body bag

Bleeding doe dies in her field of chewing gum

Eating nothing but paper wrappers and drinking bottles of rum

Shot down in the reflection of broken-down trailers and ashtrays

Tasting magnolia and penny coins till may

Bleeding doe bloody body bag hanging softly down by the trees of the bay

Dripping bottles of perfume that cuts off the airway let evergreen grown body lay

Fragile things in the arms of flowers

Taste teacups of maggots and dirty cigarettes

Ribbon tied, and a rotting rose rest

Ripping his neck backwards with the clasping of
stemmed moon flowered fingers

The smell of cigarettes and whiskey rose bud lingers

Kiss me with floral patterns twirling around like
atmosphere

Love me again like it's the 7th year

Whisper with dislocated jaw and vanilla milkshakes

While the rest of him drips and bakes

Stripped naked in the pool of overgrown rose blushed
bushes

Throw his bowels of seed out the windowpane

And let it all rot with fragile things

In the arms of flowers

Shining Over The Valley

I hope sunset is peace when death shines over the valley

The echo in my bones when the slamming of the door brings shatter to grinded bone and uses lotus to hide flowered wound

Father didn't mean to move the disturbed further into my tympanostomy tubes

So now I must cover them with tulip and daffodils

Bleed like a river of quiet waterlily over sunset of rising stars

Flooding out with gashes of moon water and valley bugs

Dead and bloomed on the field with white fence creaking

Shining over the valley body lay with skin growing flower maggots and the scent of death reeking

Eric

I hope you feel the starvation of Wilted peonies, for I am
not an easy woman to hold

Pure poetry pomegranates in the garden you spot your
digestive organs on, I would like to not sleep in the
garden tonight, I'm cold

Eric sitting on his bench throne built with rose thorns and
the teeth of his sisters

Picking off with each dry skin scrape pure purple
paradise blisters

Bleeding onto white rose and filling the well in the
garden with thick gushes of blood

I sleep with flies above the body as I feast down with
love on Eric

Flowers bleed from the mud

Poisonous

Can I please get a better taste on my lips, I don't like the grasp of poison hanging onto my kissed tongue, I'll just take small sips

Angels kiss, scorching the insides of a poison filled, better fuck forever bliss

White water, I'm swimming In lakes of shimmering fish
Can I receive the words through your larynx while our tongues fight with a poisoned stomach, making it twist?

A gagging replacement for the disgust of the rot you make me burn, your skin makes me cry and my vomit bloom with punctuated fist

Your spit poisonous, and you hit me while hate felt like a kiss

You are something I'll never miss

Scalping

I eat eyelash cluster of the food by God, plucking off one
by one as the hate that made you rape is gone

Bleed out gallons of cum matching her underwear, silk
eats brunette dead-end hair

Violated and arm disease breaks fingers, the hate you
brought will forever linger

The eyes that once rolled back to reach the skull now
dull and rotted out through the dead-end scalping's

Rip off her pubic pain and take a rape test to wash it all
off, but her scalping's are raw

Palm trees and Power lines

Sitting down on the porch, read your green book of your
hopes and lies

Palm trees, and Power lines

After sunset you'll be riding in your best friends mom's
car, windows down feeling the warm breeze fly in
through black hair

Palm trees and Power lines you drive past them while
your feelings thin and tear

You'll think of sitting down on the old porch, scorching
breeze, smoking a cigarette with your best friend, and
reading that green book, only 14.

Palm trees and Power lines you'll walk into school and
see the guy you once loved who ruined you

Who you cried over every night for an entire summer
Who gushed your heart out of your beating body

You'll have to love yourself now, but you'll still pick up
your mothers addiction, make it your new hobby

Palm trees and Power lines

You'll love your father, but hate him for leaving, so
eventually, you'll cut the power lines

You can try and smoke away the pain and fill your lungs
with the blown kiss that you imagined

Your unrequited love had given you
Just know only you can love your own hate
Not the one that holds the power line

Succubus

Blood flows through you like salt water

I can feel the delicate drip

Of seashore wash in and out, salvia on tongue to your succubus lips

Soft pink flower, delicate powder

I sniff through my nose angel dust, kiss moonlight lust

Succubus, my love for you is almost close to disgust.

Your outline shaped like pie crust,

you I must distrust

Desperate

May your watercolor blend into the sheets forever, for I do not wish to have children

I am too busy to not self-fulfill my mother's mistake

Cigarette in her left-hand cherry coke in the other

Gentle hands, dirt under nails that holds it all beneath the table where I lay under

I hid from monsters and the mirror, for my own reflection frightens me

Maple syrup above my limbs, I let it drip through the hole in the table

Pour it into my mouth, because desperately I need to feed hunger to a hostile degree

The legs on the table are wooden therefore they shall bend, do you know how to bend?

I am begging for the love I don't deserve if I do not die from hunger

I'll die from desperation

Marigold

Marigold fills orbit with passionate gold kisses

The valley filled with sunflowers maps my body, lace it with the tip of your fingers and miss this

Bouquet is a disease it is me and replaced with the blown one

You can hold another, but I know she'll never be the only one

Your vase of field flowers is filled with bugs and flies

Marigold root blooms, summertime lies.

Valentine

Kiss me sloppy, lipstick-stained love letters. I cannot feed you, for all I know is to devour

Taste it off my lips, off my mind and off my tongue

Make it drip between my legs like melted hot honey

Because when our eyes meet, you seek her twilight frame

So, I love you like a grudge, do you call me your valentine and feel ashamed?

I wear flora perfume for you, and papered bandages to hide my hair

Because underneath it lay the girl with brunette strands that locks you in her rose-colored stare

Love me like the first cut, bleed me like the first night

I love you; I promise I'll be your valentine

Ribs

I was made from the ribs that decided to beat me raw to stay

I grew berries in my womb and roses that withered from flames

While butchered body's lay in the hue of smoke, hues turned gray

May the junction of your hands bleed

Your knuckles and your fiery haze gush the color of love, for all you do is hate

You guide your fingertips across the barcode on your arm,

bleeding lakes of glittered infected rage

You devoured the wound and left nothing but rib, the one you tried to terminate

But I grew you in this womb and stitched my insides together after you left with roses

While you split apart your wrist, till the red drips lace

Strawberry aftertaste

I weep through my tears petals

While your freckled faced, ribbon laced pebbles blow heavens

Strawberry aftertaste

You'll turn me into a flower

And I'll bloom illness

Petal by petal, I was grown to love, to make love

My love making was my garden

Strawberry aftertaste on my lips of juice fleshed pink roses

By plucking my petals you don't understand beauty

Instead, you engorge yourself in dirt

Taste root and not berry

But rather it than your own hurt

Sunscreen On My Sunburnt Skin In My Field Where My House Not My Home Is

My house will be built on the field with white ribbons and ashtrays

Them Tied around my curtains with sunlight's embrace and three separate lines that separate love and like and hate

Two reasons for why I like you and love him

One reason he makes me feel like a sunburn, wet thin water on skin

Passionate about melatonin, and passionate about the taste of his limbs

Sunscreen on my sunburnt skin in my field where my house not my home Is

But he doesn't love me, instead he loves my tears

Sets flames to my fire, sets flames to my fears

But you make me feel like a thousand fires up close to my lips, nothing but the raw passionate spark of my mistake of not loving you though you still hold me to my hips

Sunscreen on my sunburnt skin in my field where my house not my home Is

You radiate honey, beauty and sin

The person I was before him

You make me burn, you make my stomach turn

But most importantly you make me feel like me and
make me want you so badly my love yearns

Sunscreen on my sunburnt skin in my field where my
house not my home Is

Missing you as if you died a bloomed blood bath

I bleed onto inks of paper, gathering my flesh and
skinning the itch in the back of my throat with tough nails

I miss you like you've died; I miss you like you've died a
bloomed bloodbath in the morning

I hope the sky will forgive you, I know the warmth won't

I know I won't

Instead, I'll forgive myself

I was Gnawing at my neck for it to spew the color of
innocence

I forgive

I forgive

I forgive

Soft flowered flow

I so badly want to be soft

Don't walk past me like another stranger

I once held the green vase that you smashed over my head, the glass bled into my fingers

The soft tenderness of the mess you brought to my arms

Now warm like green bloom season

I so badly want to be soft

You give me so many reasons

I cannot blossom like you did, and become what you hold and held

For what you held was a portion of soft honeyed lace melt

Soft drips of the suckle lightly bleeds out like flow

You drip, drip, drip, flowers hanging low

Like a soft flowered flow

Milton Keynes UK
Ingram Content Group UK Ltd.
UKHW051442250824
447237UK00021B/122

9 781998 422210